LOCOMOTION PAPERS   NUMBER ~~~

THE
USA 756th RSB
(RAILWAY SHOP BATTALION)
AT NEWPORT (Ebbw Junction)

by
E.R. Mountford

THE OAKWOOD PRESS

© The Oakwood Press 1989

ISBN 0 85361 380 X

Typeset by Gem Publishing Company, Brightwell, Wallingford, Oxfordshire
Printed by S & S Press, Abingdon, Oxfordshire

All rights reserved. No part of this book may be reproduced or transmitted in any form or by any means, electronic or mechanical, including photocopying, recording or by any information storage and retrieval system, without permission from the Publisher in writing.

Now numbered 030 TU 15, this 0–6–0 locomotive is seen at Calais shed on Tuesday, 29th August, 1961.　　　　　　　　　　　　　　　　　　　　　　Author's Collection

The late Eric Mountford

When Eric submitted this manuscript, it appeared at first glance to be of such specialised interest as to make it more appropriate for a magazine article than a book. But the more one read of it, the more one was inspired by Eric's enthusiasm for his subject and a sense of being involved in history in the making.

Because of the author's personal involvement in the story and the short timespan it covers, we have left the text very much as written because without Eric's instinctive 'feel' for history in the making and his persistence in seeking out the facts in difficult and possibly even dangerous circumstances, none of us would have appreciated the true involvement of this country in the preparation of the USA locomotives for the Invasion of Europe.

Published by
The OAKWOOD PRESS
P.O.Box 122, Headington, Oxford.

Locomotives, tank cars, and other necessary units of railroad transportation are stored up in large quantities in the British Isles ready for shipment to Europe once the invasion has begun. An Army Officer looks down at a rail yard in the 756th Railway Shop Branch, Ebbw Junction Supply Depot, where railroad locomotives are being checked before being put into storage to await issue for the invasion of the European continent (15th March, 1944).

Courtesy, US Army, Washington

This map of 1921 shows the "Three Bridges" referred to in the text (bottom left hand corner). Newport Ebbw Junction shed is below this, just off this map. Reproduced from the 1921, 25" Ordnance Survey map

The USA 756th RSB at Newport (Ebbw Jn)

The USA Locomotives "Over Here"

During World War II the railway enthusiast was, to a large extent, officially allowed to pursue his hobby peacefully, providing he did not attempt any railway photography which was, rightly, classed as a military matter. Even so, he still had to be pretty thick-skinned as, besides the opinion of the general public at the time that any railway enthusiast must be some kind of eccentric, the mere act of writing down notes in a pocket book near railway premises aroused instant suspicion and, on occasions, investigations by the authorities. At that time we were surrounded by posters, such as *Walls have ears, Say nothing that could be of use to the enemy*, so the message really hit home! People were on the look out for suspicious characters and, in the eyes of many, anyone copying down engine numbers into a note book, fell into that category.

The first half of the war period passed without anything of exceptional railway interest really happening. We (the Great Western enthusiast, that is) had lost a large number of Dean Goods 0–6–0s to the War Department, and I suppose the sight of some of those locomotives fitted with pannier tanks and also Westinghouse pumps, was something that should have tickled the palate. The GWR had mainly been compensated by the loan of 0–6–0s from the LMS and LNER but I'm afraid to me, these aroused very little interest.

My journeys by train were none too frequent, it was not just the posters, *Is your journey really necessary?* and *Must you travel?* that put one off, it was the travelling conditions themselves. There was still a vast volume of passenger traffic, mainly servicemen and women, but also businessmen short of petrol due to wartime conditions. There were also hundreds of people thronging to visit relatives and friends who lived in the cities (prone to night bombing) and a thousand and one other legitimate reasons for travelling. When a main line express was due at one of the larger stations, the platform was usually packed with people four, five and six deep, hence when the train did arrive one usually ended up jammed in the corridor. Here it was practically impossible to move as there were bodies everywhere. Some asleep, others singing in semi-inebriated stupor, and kit bags and rifles lay all over the place!

Still it was wartime, and one accepted such conditions as normal. It was on one of those wartime journeys, on Christmas Eve 1942 (travelling to spend the holiday at my Mother's home at Swindon), that I saw something that fascinated me, not just at the time, but has continued to do so. I had boarded the 12.51 pm South Wales to Paddington express at Newport, and as usual found myself huddled in the corridor, fortunately on the up side. From this side one could see the locomotives at Severn Tunnel Junction shed, also those outside the locomotive works at Swindon. On the other side there was little of interest to see between Newport and Swindon, except to count the numerous barrage balloons that filled the sky over towns, airfields and installations etc.

The train passed under the former MSWJ bridge on the western outskirts of Swindon, then alongside the old Dump sidings to the locomotive Weigh-

Locomotive No. 1604 was the first US freight locomotive to aid the War Transport effort, seen here at the hand-over ceremony at Paddington in December 1942.

British Rail

Locomotive No. 1606, seen here in March 1943 on an Ambulance train No. 11 for use by the American Army, being handed over by F.W. Hawksworth at Swindon Works, to Brig. General Hawley.

British Rail

American Engine at Paddington

RAILWAY history was made on December 11, when, for the first time, an American-built locomotive steamed into Paddington station. For the occasion it was decorated with the Stars and Stripes and the Union Jack.

This powerful freight engine was the first to arrive in London, of a batch of locomotives sent to this country from the United States to assist British railway transport.

The engine was formally handed over to Lord Leathers, Minister of War Transport, by Colonel N. A. Ryan, Chief of Transportation, American Army, who, speaking into the B.B.C. microphone, said "This, Lord Leathers, is a function that may well be recorded in history. It is my great pleasure to formally hand over to you the first American freight locomotive for use on the British Railways, and my wish is that it will do as good work for you as British engines have done already for us."

After the handing over had taken place a long blast was given on the engine whistle, to signal its official entry into service, and the ceremony concluded with the playing of the National Anthems of the United States and Great Britain.

Eight of these engines have already arrived and will be allocated to the main line railways in accordance with their requirements. They weigh 130 tons 10 cwts. with full tender and are 60 feet long. The tender carries 9 tons of coal and 5,400 gallons of water. They have a tractive effort of 31,500 lbs., and they will be used for the haulage of heavy coal and special freight trains of anything up to 1,500 tons.

Among those present were: Lord Leathers (Minister of War Transport), Mr. P. J. Noel-Baker (Joint Parliamentary Secretary, Ministry of War Transport), Major-General John C. H. Lee (Commanding General of the Services of Supply, U.S. Army, E.T.O.), Colonel N. A. Ryan (Acting Chief of Transportation Corps, U.S. Army, E.T.O.), Sir Charles Hambro (Chairman, G.W.R.), Mr. Cyril E. Lloyd (Director, G.W.R.), Sir Percy E. Bates (Director, G.W.R.), Sir Edward Cadogan (Director, G.W.R.), Sir James Milne (General Manager, G.W.R.), Mr. K. W. C. Grand (Assistant General Manager, G.W.R.), Mr. Gilbert Matthews (Superintendent of the Line, G.W.R.), Mr. F. W. Hawksworth (Chief Mechanical

U.S. ENGINE NO. 1604 AT THE HANDING OVER CEREMONY, PADDINGTON STATION.

[*Topical Press.*]

LORD LEATHERS AND COLONEL RYAN ON THE FOOTPLATE.

Lord Leathers in receiving the engine on behalf of the British Railways, said:—

"We have seen British locomotives leaving these shores for distant theatres of war, and are now seeing American locomotives arriving for service in this country.

"This engine, which I hope will be the forerunner of many more, has come at a most opportune time, just as our traffics are reaching their peak, and three years of war with steadily mounting traffic have left our fleet of locomotives inadequate to meet the demands upon it.

"This engine, which Colonel Ryan has handed over, was built in a United States shop to run on the British Railways, and I regard her as a true and tangible symbol of the co-operation of the United Nations."

Engineer, G.W.R.), Mr. F. W. Lampitt (Chief Goods Manager, G.W.R.), Sir Thomas Royden (Chairman, L.M.S.R.), Sir William V. Wood, President, L.M.S.R.), Mr. T. W. Royle (Chief Operating Manager, L.M.S.R.), Mr. W. A. Stanier (Chief Mechanical Engineer, L.M.S.R.), Sir Ronald Matthews (Chairman, L.N.E.R.), Mr. V. M. Barrington-Ward (Assistant General Manager, Operating, L.N.E.R.), Lord Ashfield (Chairman, L.P.T.B.), Mr. John Elliot (Deputy General

A page extract from the *Great Western Magazine* relating to the hand-over of the American-built locomotives.

Ebbw Junction in April 1960 with Newport locomotive shed on the left.   *Michael Hale*

Park Junction as seen in 1960.   *Michael Hale*

house, after which the mass of engines standing outside the 'A' Shop was revealed. Immediately, and whilst stretching my legs from my cramped position in preparation for alighting, I was astonished to see four USA 2–8–0s. It did not need the large USA initials on the tenders to reveal the locomotives' origin, they were unmistakenly American, exactly as we had seen in books or on films. They were numbered 1602, 1604, 1607 and 1609, and had the usual bar frames, a high pitched boiler that seemed to leave an enormous gap between the underside and the top of the motion, and a tiny chimney on the smokebox which resembled a paint tin with a rim on top. However, what stood out was what appeared to be a massive dome cover, which seemed to occupy most of the top of the boiler section which, afterwards I learned, covered a sandbox fitted in that unusual position.

The tenders seemed very large compared to the GWR tenders I was used to, and were carried on two bogies, which had solid wheels as were the pony wheels of the engines. They were painted a very dark grey, almost a light black if such colour existed, and the only lettering was the engine number painted in large numerals in the usual place on the cabside, and the "USA" on the tender. Despite my initial description there was a very neat line about them; the designers had made them impressive looking machines, in spite of the pipes and fittings on the outside, and I personally found them both pleasing and intriguing.

The sight of these engines had come as a complete surprise. Naturally, at the height of wartime, nothing had been written in the press about the arrival of USA engines in this country, although the railway press reported soon afterwards that one of the engines, No. 1604, had been involved in a handing-over ceremony at Paddington Station on 11th December, 1942. The locomotive, decked out in the flags of the two nations, was formally handed over by Colonel N.A. Ryan of the US Army to Lord Leathers, the Minister of War Transport. After the ceremony the engine returned to Swindon Works, where modifications took place before it was officially added to GWR stock on 28th December.

From the records it appears that No. 1604 was one of four similar engines (possibly more) that were landed at Cardiff Docks on 27th November, believed to be the first to arrive in this country. The first to be lifted from the ship to the quay was No. 1609, the Cardiff East Dock shed breakdown gang being sent to the Queen Alexandra Dock to assist the unloading.

During the following months large numbers of the American 'S160' Class, as they were designated, arrived in this country, the first 400 being allocated to the big four railways. The allocations varied slightly but basically the GWR had 174, the LNER 170, the LMS 50 and the SR — who were reasonably well off for motive power due to the loss of traffic to the southern ports — had 6. In these circumstances it is surprising that I did not see another 'S160', and the first actually working a train, until 4th June, 1943, when No. 1881 passed through Newport on a down goods. After that, they appeared with increasing frequency. The GWR shed code to which each engine was allocated, was stencilled on the small bracket, over the pony wheels — immediately behind the front buffer beam. During June I noted Nos. 1609 and 1616 were PPRD (Pontypool Road), 1894 NPT (Ebbw Jn Newport), 1897

OXF (Oxford), and 1893 STJ (Severn Tunnel Jn). There were many others but the codes soon became indistinct due to grime except at close quarters. The engines became so much part of the railway scene that scarcely an eyebrow was raised as one passed through a station.

Soon after this, on 30th August, 1943, I glanced from my dining room window in Newport, across to the railway, some quarter-of-a-mile distant at the bottom of the hill. Held by a signal at East Usk Junction was a short train of two of the American 2–8–0s, being hauled by another engine of the same class. I hastily jumped on my bicycle, and cycled to a suitable vantage point. The train engine was one of those on loan to the GWR, No. 2149, which was hauling the two dead locomotives Nos. 2320 and 2281, both of which had their cabs boarded up. There was a small open wagon between the train engine and No. 2320, and also between the two dead locomotives, and at the rear was a standard GWR mineral brake van.

The importance of this sighting did not register immediately, one is always prepared for the unusual in wartime, but a few days later, on 9th September, I saw another similar train at the same spot, the train engine was No. 2110, hauling three dead engines Nos. 1678, 2594 and 2807. This made me realise something of importance was taking place somewhere in South Wales, although I did not realise it would be so close to where I lived, such was the secrecy in wartime.

The 'S160' 2–8–0s at Ebbw Jn

A few days later I was riding my bicycle westwards along the Cardiff Road, in Newport. Approaching Maesglas, and close to the lane that led to Ebbw Junction shed, were three bridges over the road. The first of these carried the Western Valley line to Newport Dock Street and area, the second carried the curved link line (known as the Western Loop) from the South Wales main line at Ebbw Junction to the Western Valley line at Park Junction. The third, or the most western of the three bridges carried the former Alexandra (Newport and South Wales) Docks and Railway (ADR for short) line from the Brecon & Merthyr junction at Bassaleg to Newport Docks. Immediately west of the third bridge were ADR sidings that looked down on to suburban back gardens. On the up side of these sidings stood two or three rows of the gaunt USA 2–8–0s, obviously waiting entry to Ebbw Junction shed. I believe the official name of the sidings was "Docks Up Sidings", but I did not know it at the time and I referred to them as Three Bridges sidings, a name I have used ever since.

The problem was how to find out, under wartime conditions, what was happening. Although railways (or Railway) were in my blood from birth, and I had served my locomotive apprenticeship at Swindon, I was not working for the railways during the war, hence did not have the advantage of being on the inside at Ebbw Junction, so it was a tricky problem. However, my curiosity and the sense of history overcame my caution and on Sunday 17th October I cycled down to Ebbw shed, propped my bicycle against the red brick watchman's office that guarded the road entrance, and started wandering over towards the sidings. It was then I had my next surprise, as

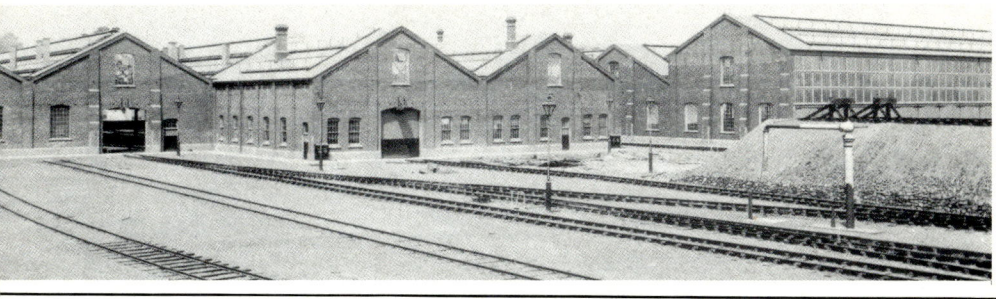

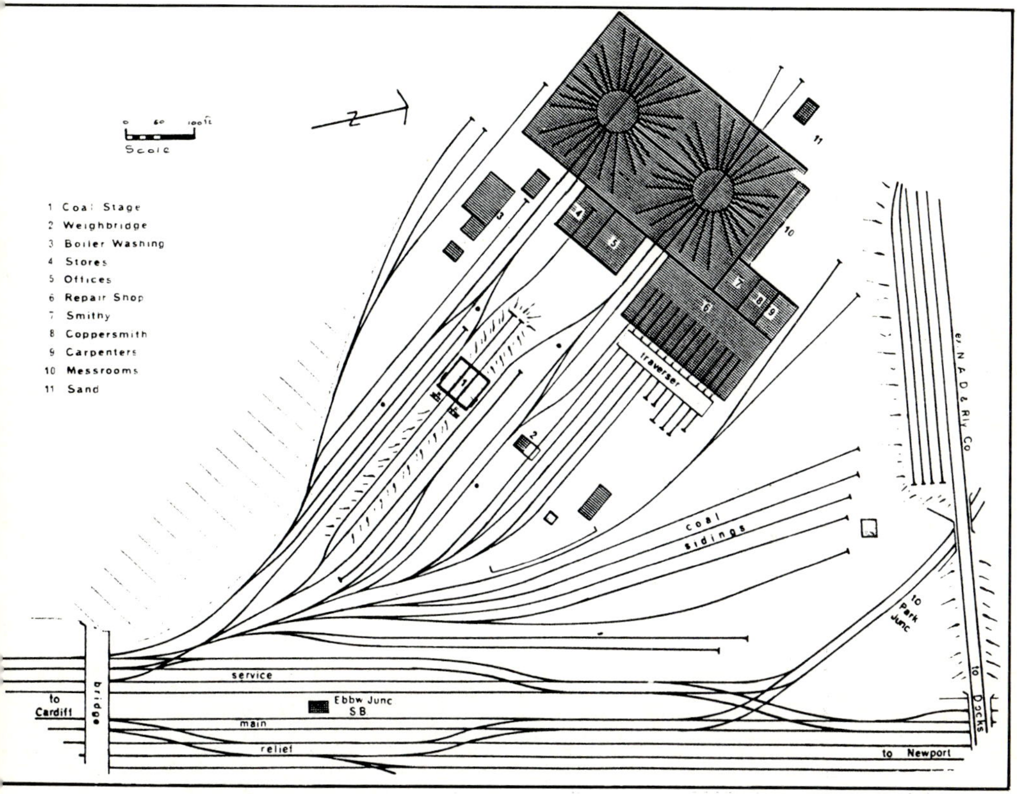
Scale
1 Coal Stage
2 Weighbridge
3 Boiler Washing
4 Stores
5 Offices
6 Repair Shop
7 Smithy
8 Coppersmith
9 Carpenters
10 Messrooms
11 Sand
traverser
coal sidings
to Park Junc
to Docks
to Newport
to Cardiff
bridge
service
main
relief
Ebbw Junc SB

Newport Ebbw Jn shed track layout. *Courtesy E. Lyons*

Newport Ebbw Jn Shed replaced a small four-road shed on a cramped site at Newport High Street and opened on 17th July, 1915. Built to a similar pattern to the larger shed at Old Oak Common, the two roundhouses were built with provision for two further roundhouses to be added at the rear, should the need have arisen. A large repair shop was able to deal with locomotives on 12 roads and was 'fed' by a 35 ton traverser. The depot closed on 11th October, 1965 and was quickly demolished, a new diesel depot opening a short distance westwards on 5th December, 1965.

USA locomotive being unloaded at Cardiff Docks. No date was available and the photograph was censored by "control" stamped on it. *Author's Collection*

No. 2148, 2–8–0 USA locomotive on a long freight train near Oxford. *R.H.G. Simpson*

Another test train officially photographed "somewhere in the Country" in 1943 with USA 2–8–0s Nos. 2148 and 1892 in charge. *British Rail*

USA/TC class 'S160' 2–8–0 No. 1604 on a test coal train at Rogerstone in May 1943.
British Rail

A line of American 2–8–0s at Swindon Works on 22nd January, 1943 with No. 1619 nearest the camera. *British Rail*

No. 2159, 2–8–0 USA locomotive. *Lens of Sutton*

there were far more of the 2–8–0s then I had imagined stored on sidings east of the main line, which were on the continuation of the ADR lines already mentioned. This line (after passing over the Cardiff Road bridge) fanned out into a similar set of sidings east of that bridge, which terminated at a small bridge which passed over the Cardiff curve line from Ebbw Junction. There were no USA engines on those sidings which were still being used for wagons. The ADR lines then passed over a very long bridge over the GWR main line and numerous sidings, after which they again fanned out into the massive West Mendalgief sidings, which terminated not all that far from the former ADR Pill locomotive shed (see map on page 4).

It was on three of the up side West Mendalgief sidings that a large number of the 2–8–0s were stored. Neither these nor Three Bridges sidings had any direct access to Ebbw shed and engines from either, destined for the shed, would have to be towed to the junction (just beyond Park Junction) and back down the Cardiff curve to Ebbw, a total distance of about a mile from West Mendalgief sidings. I did not venture too far around the sidings that day, but recorded 42 of the 'S160s' before retreating. Whilst doing so I saw No. 1913 returning tender first around the loop mentioned, and concluded it was returning from a trial trip. I was not seriously challenged on this unauthorised prowl, and managed to gather that the US Army had taken over the lifting/fitting shop on the west side of Ebbw Junction shed, and it was there that the US engines were being dealt with.

Because of compulsory regular overtime and as a member of the AFS (Auxiliary Fire Service) with night standby duty, and frequent air raid alerts (heralded by that awful haunting sound of the local sirens), I could not get down to Ebbw shed again for nearly a fortnight. But, on the morning of Sunday, 29th October, I again cycled to the shed and, after depositing the bicycle, strolled boldly into the main shed, around the turntable, and into the fitting shop (via the little door in the corner, the only direct entrance from the main shed). I walked over to the nearest American soldier (do they call them soldiers — engineers, sappers, etc.?) and asked if he would kindly direct me to the officer-in-charge.

Near the doorway mentioned was a typical small GWR shop office, reached by a small flight of steps, from which the supervisor was able to survey the whole of his domain from above. Apparently that office and most of the shop had been taken over by the 756th Railway Shop Battalion (RSB) of the US Transportation Corps, commanded by Major E.C. Hanly. The Major was not present on my visit and I met his second-in-command, a Lt Walters. Crossing my fingers (not only for luck, but also to get a grip on my nerves) I explained my deep interest in railway locomotives, taking care to mention that I had been trained as a locomotive fitter, turner and erector at Swindon, a works which even the American respected at the time, and that I was particularly interested in this new development to my locomotive knowledge. Lt Walters was a youngish, pleasant man who treated me more as a fellow locomotive engineer, and not as an enthusiast, which part I had carefully played down but not deleted entirely. He took me around the fitting shop, the east end of which had a small but efficient machine section. He told me that the 756 RSB had started at Ebbw Junction on 14th September, 1943, on which day there were 104 of the 2−8−0s either stored at the two sites previously referred to, or in the fitting shop yard, whilst a further six were in the shop ready for operations to commence.

The shop contained twelve pits, the first two from the office were connected directly from the yard sidings but the other ten could only be reached via a traversing table which ran outside the shop. The next four pits were accessible from the yard via the traverser, but there were only dead end sidings on the opposite side of the table to the last six pits. The 756 RSB were allotted the first ten pits, leaving the last two for the GWR to carry out light repairs that could not be handled in the main shed; normally a heavy lifting job, as a 35 ton overhead gantry crane ran the length of the shop. On 29th October there were five US engines in the shop, Nos. 2173, 2175, 2176, 2614 and 2112. The latter was one of the 2−8−0s on loan to the GWR and was on one of the last two pits, the others were on the "US pits" and being dealt with by their own soldiers. Normally there were five, sometimes six, locomotives on the "US pits", their other pits being occupied by small open wagons containing rods, spares and stores etc. The engines arrived with the sides and backs of the cabs boarded up, and outside rods removed for towing. After the timber had been removed and the rods refitted, the engines were given a thorough inspection, and then greased and oiled as necessary. They were then taken into the yard, coaled and watered and steamed for their trial run.

When ready, a GWR driver and fireman from the main shed, accompanied on the footplate by a US Army NCO, took the engine around the Western curve, through Bassaleg Junction and on to either Rogerstone or Risca, on the Western Valley line. If all was well, the engine was transferred to the main shed on return, where it passed temporarily to GWR control to enable it to undertake a trial under working conditions, usually handling a freight train with a return mileage of approximately 300. When it returned from the second trial it was handed back to the 756 RSB, put in the shop again, the cab partially boarded in again and, after a liberal supply of grease, was put to store in readiness for the awaited invasion of Europe. Details of this second storage will be given later on.

Reverting to 29th October, I did not push my luck further by asking Lt Walters if I could visit the two pre-shop storage sites, but whilst in the yard I did see No. 2170 returning light engine, tender first, from its initial trial trip to Risca. Until the US Army arrived on the scene there had been no direct connection from the fitting shop yard to the Cardiff curve, only from the main shed sidings, but with dead engine movements and also trial trips several times daily, a direct link was added on 17th October, 1943. The loan of after-trial engines to the main shed for the working trial was most welcome, as normally it made at least three, often four, extra heavy freight engines available. They were usually used on goods/mineral trains to the Midlands, or to the London area, but also to West Wales and sometimes even to the West of England.

I first saw one of the 'S160s' with its tender lettered "Transportation Corps" in small lettering, immediately above the normal "USA" letters on the 22nd September. The locomotive was No. 2440, one of those on loan to the GWR, which was working an up goods through Newport. Such lettering soon became commonplace, and could be seen on the tenders of both Army engines and the GWR batch. Even so, right up until the engines left this country, the majority still carried the "USA" lettering only.

By October it was far from easy to be certain which of the 2–8–0s were Army engines, and which were on loan, particularly at Ebbw Junction where there were always quite a number of both groups. In the main shed it was common to see several of the class occupying pits around the turntable, some were Army engines ready for their "GWR trial", others were identical engines on loan. Individual engine numbers did not help either, as the groups were not divided by numerical batches, but purely by the date they had arrived in this country. The first locomotives were on loan to the big four railways, whilst later arrivals were purely Army engines, to be held in readiness for immediate use in Europe following the Invasion. Even in the fitting shop there could usually be seen one or two engines of the GWR loan batch, standing alongside the Army engines. Apart from the clean/unused look of the latter, the only notable difference was that US army engineers were working on their engines, whilst GWR fitters were repairing the engines on loan. Even in the yards, both GWR and US sections, the same could often be seen in the fitting shop yard, as it was normally a "GWR" USA 2–8–0 that would be restored to assemble and tow the Army engines to their final storage site. It was all very confusing to those of us "not fully in the know".

I paid a brief visit to the fitting shop on Saturday 13th November, to meet Major Hanly. Although I entered both the shed and shop with far more confidence in the knowledge that contact had already been made, I could not help feeling somewhat uneasy as to how the Major would view my presence. However, Lt Walters had broken the ice and my brief chat with the Major confirmed that he had no objection to my visits providing I was shepherded by the Lieutenant, and not allowed to know too much of what was going on. I obtained the Major's blessing for a complete visit to the shop and sidings on 28th November.

I thought it best, at that stage, not to ask to visit the final storage site as, on reflection, a "student of locomotives" could hardly claim to derive much benefit from looking at a dump of stored engines, however exciting this might be to the enthusiast. In that connection I heard — or thought I heard — the name Panteg mentioned by a couple of the soldiers hence the following Saturday morning, 20th November, I caught the local train to Panteg. Once there, I wandered across that very lengthy bridge that spanned the Newport to Hereford main line, and numerous sidings, a short distance south of Pontypool Road station. I looked in vain for S160s, but my only reward was one solitary member of the class heading northwards on a goods train.

When I paid the planned visit to Ebbw Junction on 28th November I was still under the impression that I had gone to the correct place to see the stored 2–8–0s, but that they must have been on some of the numerous sidings in that area not visible from the bridge. I told Lt Walters of my abortive visit to which he gave a broad grin remarking, "No wonder, they are at Tonteg not Panteg". I persuaded him to approach Major Hanly on my

American 2–8–0 Austerity locomotives stored on the Barry Railway line at Treforest in 1944. There were 119 locomotives all in one long line. *Author's Collection*

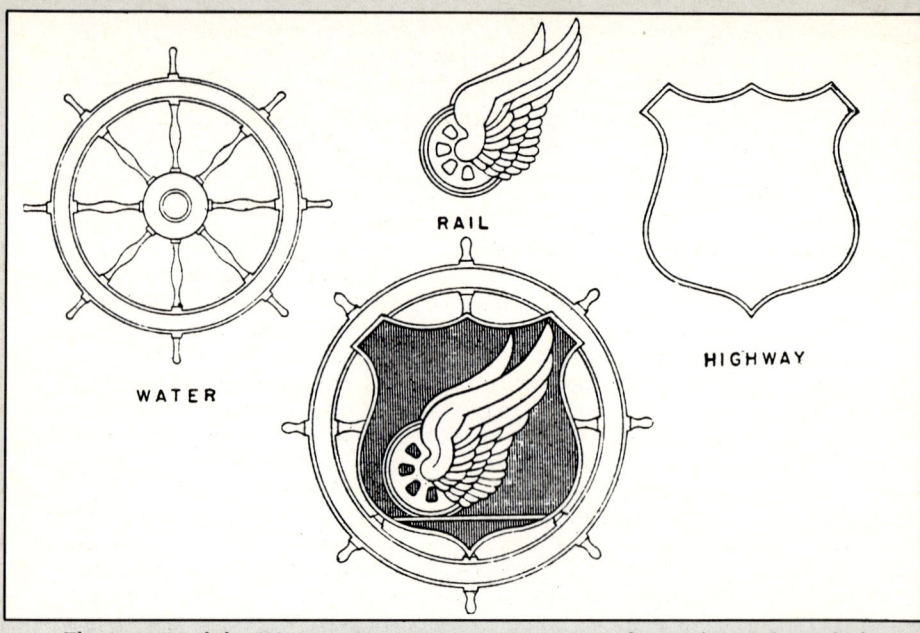

The insignia of the US Army Transportation Corps is made up of an eight spoked ship's wheel (representing ports, port battalions, harbour craft companies etc); the shield of the familiar USA highway marker (symbolising lorry companies and highway controllers) and the winged wheel (representing the Military Railways Service). The insignia as a whole denote the efficiency and coordination of water, road and rail transport for military purposes.

```
                    HEADQUARTERS
            DET. "E" 756TH RAILWAY SHOP BN.
                     A.P.O. 516

                                          9 December 1943.

SUBJECT: Builders Number and Builders Specification Card on
         locomotives stored at Tonteg.

TO      : Corporal of the Guard, Tonteg.

     1. This will be your authority to permit Mr. E. R. Mountford to
walk along the left side of locomotives stored at Tonteg to see the
Builders Numbers and Builders Specification Placards.

     2. In no way should he be permitted to secure information of the
total locomotives stored at Tonteg and he must be accompanied by the
Guard at all times.

                                          Edwin C. Hanly
                                          EDWIN C. HANLY,
                                          MAJOR,       TC.
                                          Commanding
```

The official pass for the author to visit Tonteg.

behalf to grant me a permit to visit the Tonteg site, which he promised to do before my next visit. However, let us first deal with the 28th November when, at last I felt relaxed to stroll around the shop, yard and sidings at will with official blessing. In the fitting shop that day were Nos. 2616, 2569, 2615, 2574, 2840 and 2804. The one nearest the office, No. 2616 was in steam and Lt Walters took me on the footplate and explained the various controls in detail. However, this is not intended as a technical story, such details are readily available, hence I will confine my notes to observations made.

By that date the shop was dealing with the engines faster than they were arriving from the ports, hence I only recorded a total of 61 of the 'S160s' that day. Of these, 21 were stored at Three Bridges sidings, twenty at Mendalgief sidings, and fourteen were in the fitting shop yard, the other six in the shop as listed above. In the yard was a small four-wheeled diesel shunter which was being used by the 756 RSB as the yard pilot. It did not carry a maker's plate, but was numbered D5 and lettered "USA Transportation Corps". It certainly did not look powerful enough to be constantly moving several of the heavy 2−8−0s from the local pre-shop storage sites to the yard. Its main problem — I was later told — was that it was frequently derailed particularly in the yard sidings, which must have proved a serious problem with such a rapid flow of engines in/out of shop. I never saw it again, and have been unable to find any details about it.

Storage at the Tonteg site

I picked up my pass to visit Tonteg on a brief visit I paid to Ebbw Junction on 9th December. I did not visit the yard or sidings that day, but in the shop were Nos. 1685, 1686, 1756, 1791, 1796 and 1798. The pass had been typed and signed by Major Hanly personally. I was told to report to the US Army NCO immediately, be accompanied by the guard, at all times, and must walk on the left side of the locomotives only. Also, whilst I could note particulars from the Makers' Specification Plates, on no account must I be allowed to know the total number of engines stored at Tonteg. This latter condition seemed a bit odd to me, as I could not see how I could record all the locomotive numbers and makers' details without knowing how many engines were there. Still I was not one to argue about something entirely in my favour, hence two days later on Saturday, 11th December I set off for Tonteg little knowing what to expect. In those days I did not know the Tonteg area very well, and I could not visualise any group of sidings capable of storing a large number of big tender engines. I knew there were the former TVR/Barry Railway exchange sidings near the junction at Treforest, but thought that these were still used, and in any case they would hardly have been classified as Tonteg.

I caught a main line train Newport to Cardiff then the local "auto" to Pontypridd, via St Fagans. On arrival at Tonteg Halt (a secluded spot), I was the only one to alight on that bitterly cold and frosty morning. The "auto" disappeared down the bank to Treforest (TVR) and there I stood with not an engine in sight, let alone one from the USA. Fortunately there was a small signal cabin, Tonteg Junction. I hailed the signalman and enquired the location of the American engines. Without hesitation, he pointed a hand

Soldiers of the 756th Railway Shop Bn, guard a concentration of Army locomotives at Ebbw Junction. These engines were to be used for the operations against the European continent (15th March, 1944).

Courtesy, US Army, Washington

along the old Barry line to Pontypridd and the Rhondda, and said, "They're just around the corner, walk on and you'll soon come to them".

On going "around the corner" (i.e. the line followed the natural curvature of the hillside), I saw a sight never to be forgotten and never likely to be repeated. There stretched out before me was a seemingly never-ending line of the 2–8–0s, buffer to buffer, chimneys facing northwards, the locomotives curving around the ledge cut into the hillside as far as the eye could see. That was the answer; there were no sidings, the US Army had taken over the up line completely, leaving the down line still in use as a single line section. No wonder I had been instructed to walk on the left side of the locomotives, the right rail was the running rail and still in use for coal traffic by the GWR.

When I reached the first engine, No 2574, my problems began. There was no sign of any American soldiers, or indeed of any living thing, hence I was unable to comply with the "report on arrival" condition. This was somewhat worrying as, despite my permit, tales were rife that some US soldiers were "trigger happy", and I did not relish being fired at. Next, I could see no way of walking on the left side of the engines. The Barry Railway had literally cut a ledge into the hillside on which they laid the lines to the Rhondda and almost from the far edge of the sleepers the hillside continued to climb, making walking on that side extremely difficult, to say the least.

Therefore I decided to walk the live track, keeping alert not only for a possible coal train, but also for any US soldier whose hobby back at home may have been hunting. I slowly plodded the single line track, noting the number and building details of each engine as I slipped and slithered on the frosty wooden sleepers. The 32nd engine from the Tonteg end, No. 2160, unlike all the others was chimney southwards, and I mused why just one locomotive in such a vast line should be facing the opposite direction to all the others.

Just over halfway along the massive line I reached the old Barry station at Treforest, closed to passengers in May 1930, but then reasonably intact. I climbed aboard one locomotive and got down on the up platform and surveyed the scene from that side. At least for a moment I was walking the correct side, as instructed, but shortly after leaving the platform I had to get back on the other side, and continued there until the end of the line. It was bitterly cold, and I had a job to hold the pencil in one hand and the notebook in the other, as the inclination was to rub my hands together for warmth. As I glanced down into the Taff Valley I noticed the smoke lazily rising from the chimneys of the houses below, and thought of the occupants enjoying the warmth from their open fires, whilst I risked near-frostbite and the chance of being shot at, just so I could walk alongside a line of dead engines. Still, my enthusiasm and the sense of history carried me on. The hazy sunshine bravely shone on the glistening sleepers, without any hope of thawing them out as I ambled on until the last engine, No. 2616, was reached, her chimney just outside the south end of Treforest Tunnel, the other end of which opened out to the old Pontypridd Graig Station. Blue with cold, but exhilarated at what I had seen, I mused about 2606 and her travels since leaving the Baldwin Locomotive Works in July. It had made the perilous Atlantic crossing as deck cargo, survived the lurking submarines, and had been landed safely at London Docks on 8th September. The same day it had commenced its long journey to Ebbw Junction being towed with Nos. 2599 and 2808 down the GWR main line to Swindon, and thence around the Gloucester route to South Wales, as lines of dead engines were not allowed through the Severn Tunnel. It arrived at Ebbw the next day, and during the following four weeks it had passed through the USA/TC shop twice, undertaken its US and GWR trial trips and been towed to Tonteg with Nos. 2827 and 2599 on 11th October. I did not know it then, but 2606 was destined to stand there at the tunnel mouth until 8th September, 1944, almost exactly one year since it was unloaded at London Docks, before setting off on her travels through the war zones of Europe to end up after the war on the stock of the Hungarian State Railways.

Still that is jumping ahead. On that bleak Saturday morning in December 1943 I had reached the end of the line and not set eyes on one US soldier and, better still from my point of view, not one US soldier had set eyes on me. On the down side at the tunnel mouth was a small platelayer's hut, a tell-tale wisp of smoke drifting from its solitary chimney, indicating that I had found life at last. Since I had left Tonteg, just over one and a half miles away and two hours ago, I had not seen or spoken to a soul, nor had a train passed along the single line.

I opened the door of the hut and inside were four American soldiers sitting at a table drinking coffee and playing cards. The hut was lovely and warm, the fire blazing and there was that homely smell of fresh coffee. I'm not sure who was the most surprised, the guards or me. However, I quickly announced that I had a permit from Major Hanly to have a look around the engines, to which the Corporal replied, "They're all out there, friend, but have a cup of coffee first." The coffee was superb, and I hardly had the heart to say that I had seen everything already as I had started from the other end of the line. However, the Corporal seemed somewhat relieved at that and, after producing my permit, I sat down and thoroughly enjoyed a chat with them whilst thawing out. I soon had to leave to trudge back up the line to Tonteg Halt and my return train. The US guards did not accompany me, I left them in the platelayer's hut.

On arrival home I naturally broke the final condition of my permit and counted up the number of engines in the line at Tonteg — 119. I wonder if this was the longest line of engines ever assembled in this country, or indeed elsewhere? As each engine was 61 ft 0¼ in. in length from buffer to buffer, the total length of the "locomotive line" was 1 mile 660½ yards plus a few extra yards for the bridges and footpaths which were left clear. It was certainly the greatest railway spectacle I have seen in my sixty years as an enthusiast. At the time it made me realise that nothing was being left to chance in the preparation for the invasion of Europe. I paid a further visit to Tonteg early in January 1944, but the position was unchanged, evidently the site was considered to be full.

Fresh arrivals at Ebbw Jn

My next visit to Ebbw Junction, which due to changed circumstances proved to be my last for several months, took place on 9th January, 1944 and was the most interesting of all. On my previous visits the 756 RSB had been dealing solely with the 2–8–0s of the 'S160' class. Although there were sixteen of the class still at Three Bridges sidings, and a further ten at West Mendalgief sidings, flanked on either side of the latter on this visit were two lines of USA 0–6–0Ts, fifteen on siding No. 5 and eighteen on No. 7.

These comprised Nos. 1302–1316, 1932–1936, 1947–1951 and 4372–4380, apart from No. 1307 which was in steam and being used as the fitting shop pilot, in place of the mysterious diesel (now disappeared) No. D5. The yard and shop contained a further 23 of the 2–8–0s. The 0–6–0T certainly seemed far more powerful for the pilot job, despite looking somewhat ungainly, and typically American. The wheels were bunched together to obtain the short wheelbase necessary to negotiate curves as little as 150 ft radius, whilst the boiler and tanks were again pitched high and well clear of the motion. The boiler had what seemed to be three dome covers, and the cab was massive, spoiled to some extent by a diminutive bunker. Apart from No. 1307 the others still had their cabs boarded up from the sea crossing, as did the 2–8–0s.

Tank engines of this class had started to arrive in this country in the Summer of 1942, and the first batches were put to work mainly on the military railways, Longmoor, Melbourne, etc. The 34 that I saw at Ebbw had been mostly landed at Cardiff Docks, in December 1943, and appeared to be intended for testing by the 756 RSB, and then stored for overseas use like the 2–8–0s.

The tank engines were not the only surprise of my visit on 9th January. In the USA yard stood three double-ended diesel locomotives with central cabs, carrying the numbers 7963–7965, the number being in a small rectangular frame, four in all mounted at each front top corner of the bonnets. We were not used to diesels in South Wales, our only experience being the AEC/GWR railcars introduced in 1934. The GWR had a handful of 0–6–0 diesel shunters, used in the London and Bristol areas, but the USA diesels were main line machines with the 0–4–4–0 wheel arrangement, completely different to the GWR diesels mentioned. They had been constructed by the Whitcomb Loco. Co. in October 1943, and were painted a sandy colour because (so I was told) they were intended for desert use in North Africa. They had a searchlight headlamp in the centre at each end, and a bell fixed on the right side in front of the driving cab. The latter was quite luxurious compared to our steam engines, with a comfortable fixed armchair for the driver.

One other item of interest that day was the "discovery" in the fitting shop office of a notebook, made up by Major Hanly, recording each locomotive as it passed through the shop. It had four simple columns only, the progressive number, engine number, date into shop and date completed. A total of 224 of the 2–8–0s had been dealt with when I saw the book, the last entry being No. 2586 completed on 7th January, 1944. How I regret never seeing that book again, it would have saved years of research, and would have been

Tank cars and freight cars concentrated at Ebbw Junction until they were used to transport quantities of men and material in support of the invasion of Europe (7th April, 1944). *Courtesy, US Army, Washington*

Empty 40 ton US-built rail tank wagons wait for their movement to France. These tanks had a capacity of 9000 gallons and were 40 ft 9¾ in. long. The tanks, bogies minus wheels and axles, the axleboxes, wheels and axles and side buffers and drawgear were all shipped separately and the components put together here.

complete and reliable. Possibly it survived to get into US military records somewhere; it would be a mine of information if ever found.

However, from that visit onwards we must rely, to some extent, on an old semi-official notebook that came to light some twenty years afterwards, along with the occasional sighting I was able to make during that crucial year, 1944.

Two further storage sites are necessary

Once the Tonteg site was full, a second storage site was chosen formerly belonging to the Barry Railway, being the Barry/Rhymney exchange sidings between the old Penrhos Lower and Upper Junctions. These sidings had mainly fallen into disuse following the 1922 amalgamations, the coal trains proceeding direct from the collieries to the dock storage sidings. The Penrhos site consisted of four double ended sidings on each side of the double track Barry's Rhymney branch, the sidings themselves being just over a quarter of a mile in length. Although the notebook referred to failed to record a handful of the 'S160s' stored at Penrhos, all available evidence points to there being no less than 152 of them put to store on the eight sidings between December 1943 and February 1944. Despite being spread out compared with the Tonteg site, Penrhos had been carefully chosen. The sidings were sited in a natural break in the hillside between the Rhymney and Taff valleys in an area well wooded, little inhabited, and only approachable along country lanes. The engines would have been hardly visible from the air, particularly at night when air raids could be expected.

By the end of February the Penrhos site, was full, and so a third site had to be found. Those "in the know" must have been aware that the invasion was not far off as, unlike the first two sites hidden away on not-too-busy mineral lines, the third site — at Cadoxton — was just about as public as it could be. The frequent Barry to Cardiff commuter service actually passed between the lines of 2–8–0s in this case, there for all to see. The actual site was almost immediately east of Cadoxton Junction, where two sets of dead-end sidings fanned out each side of the main line, terminating at the embankment for the Palmerston Road bridge, just west of Biglis Junction with the Taff Vale's Penarth branch.

Although the records at this site are not as complete as at Tonteg and Penrhos, it seems reasonably clear that 84 of the 2–8–0s were stored there. A couple more were recorded as having passed through Ebbw shops, but appear to have been sent for overseas duty direct, and not put into store. The Cadoxton site was almost completed in April 1944, but there were a few late arrivals in May. A full list of the engines stored at each site is given in Appendix One, meanwhile, a description of the route taken by the engines to reach the storage sites is given below. These are particularly interesting in relation to the number of pre-grouping companies' lines the engines had to pass over. A GWR engine hauled the locomotives in each case, although this was normally an 'S160' from the allocated batch. In the early stages it was four, sometimes three, engines towed together in one batch, although towards the end at Cadoxton, there were often only two 2–8–0s behind the train engine.

To the Tonteg Site (c.20¾ miles)	Distance M C	Former Rly
Ebbw Junction (via Western Curve)–Park Junction	0–56	GWR
Park Junction–Bassaleg Junction	1–12	GWR (Western Valley)
Bassaleg Junction (via Machen)–Caerphilly East Junction	9–13	B & M Rly
Caerphilly East Junction–Penrhos Junction	1–02	Rhymney Rly
Penrhos Junction–PC&N Junction Pontypridd	5–12	A(N&SW)D Rly
PC&N Junction–Treforest Junction	0–74	Taff Vale Rly
Treforest Junction–Tonteg Junction	1–54	Barry Rly
Tonteg Junction–Storage site (average)	1–75	Barry Rly

To the Penrhos Site (c.12½ miles)	Distance M C	Former Rly
Ebbw Junction–Penrhos Junction (as above)	12–3	As above
Penrhos Junction–Storage Site (Say)	0–40	Barry Rly

To the Cadoxton Site (c.16¾ miles)	Distance M C	Former Rly
Ebbw Junction (via Relief line to Cardiff)–Penarth Curve South Junction	11–07	GWR
Penarth Curve South Junction–Cogan Junction	1–61	Taff Vale Rly
Cogan Junction–Cadoxton Junction	3–57	Barry Rly
Cadoxton Junction–Storage site (Say)	0–20	Barry Rly/GWR

A GWR official Minute, shortly after the War, recorded that 355 of the American 2–8–0s were stored in South Wales, which tends to confirm the totals of 119 at Tonteg, 152 at Penrhos, and 84 at Cadoxton, However, three other 'S160s' passed through the USA/TC shop at Ebbw during that initial stage. The first was No. 2639 which had its trial run on 4th January, but was allocated to the Longmoor Military Railway. I was fortunate to see it heading eastwards through Newport Station on a goods train on 14th January, presumably from which it transferred to Longmoor. Two others, Nos. 2264 and 2858, were late arrivals in April, and which, after shopping and trials, were amongst twelve engines despatched by the 756 RSB towards the South Coast, between 2nd May and 5th May, in readiness for overseas duty.

American 0–6–0Ts and Diesel locomotives

Now a word about the 0–6–0Ts dealt with at Ebbw Junction. The initial 34 were quickly followed by further batches, Nos. 1945/6, 1976–1987, 2000/1, 4313–4338, 4381–4401, 6000–3/5/7–9/15/6 and 6162–6166, another 78 engines. Eight of these, Nos. 1977/80/4 and 4319/26/87/91/4, were not recorded in the notebook, but there is some evidence that most, if not all, went to Ebbw initially for the weather boarding to be removed, and for steam trial. None were stored at Three Bridges sidings prior to shopping as far as I know, they were always at West Mendalgief sidings or in the shop yard. All arrived fairly early in 1944, and after trial 24 were loaned to the GWR in the South Wales area, whilst one or two others were used at US Military Installations — one was at Barry. The trial of these engines was carried out in, and around, the shop yard, on pilot duty as far as possible. They never went out for a trial on the running lines as did the 2–8–0s.

Although some had already been on loan to the GWR for a short time the official loan date was 7th June, 1944. Nos. 1945/6/76/8/81/3/5 were working in the Cardiff Valleys Division (shedded at Cardiff East Dock, Barry and Radyr) Nos. 4381/3–5/8–90/2/3/5/7/8 in the Newport Division (Ebbw Junction and Pill) whilst Nos. 1307 and 1987 (Dyffryn Yard) with 4399 and 4401 (Danygraig) were in the Neath Division. Of these Nos. 4385 and 4398 were transferred to the Victoria and Albert Docks, London on 6th July, whilst No. 1983 did little work on the GWR as it was stopped for repair at Radyr Shed on 21st June, had to wait for shopping at Barry Works until 31st July, and not set to work until 12th August. Those on loan were returned to the USA/TC at Ebbw Junction between 29th August and 8th September inclusive from where, after inspection, they were despatched to embarkation ports in France.

Apart from one or two retained at the yard for pilot duties, the 0–6–0Ts not out on loan, were despatched for storage to Duffryn Isaf sidings, sited between Bedwas and Maesycwmmer on the former Brecon and Merthyr section. Once again these were redundant exchange sidings, between the Barry and B&M Railways. The sidings were on the west side of the B&M line, sited at the eastern end of the former massive Llanbradach Viaduct (demolished in 1937) by which the Barry had spanned the Rhymney Valley to achieve access to the coal mined alongside the B&M system. The engines stored at the site followed the same route from Ebbw Junction to Machen (6 m 69 ch) as did the 2–8–0s en route to Toneg or Penrhos, but from Machen they continued along the B&M main line for the 4 m 37 ch to Duffryn Isaf, a total distance of some 11¼ miles. The sidings were but a short distance north-east of the town of Caerphilly, whilst the Penrhos site was similarly just south-west of the town.

Unfortunately the small notebook did not record the 0–6–0Ts as they were taken to Duffryn Isaf (in May and June 1944) but it did contain some sketchy records of some of the engines leaving the site in August, prior to despatch overseas. However, from observations of local inhabitants, it is estimated that between 60 and 80 engines were there.

Finally, some details of the diesels which, although more fully documented than the 0–6–0Ts, are incomplete. The official total put to store was 65, which almost certainly covered the following batches:

Whitcomb	650 hp	0–4–4–0DE	Nos. 7961–7980, 8120–8129
GEC	500 hp	0–4–4–0DE	Nos. 7228–7237, 7924–7929
GEC	380 hp	0–4–4–0DE	Nos. 8499–8509, 8521–8528

Nine of the above were not mentioned in the notebook. Of these Nos.

Locomotive No. 1413 0–6–0 showing a different livery to that on the locomotive in the view below. *Lens of Sutton*

Locomotive No. 4372, 0–6–0, at Newbury Dump in 1945. *Author's Collection*

7966/73/6/9 are known to have gone to Longmoor, but may well have gone to Ebbw Junction beforehand for initial examination and trial. The others, Nos. 7234/6, 7926/9 and 8504, are not accounted for, but almost certainly passed through Ebbw. Most of the diesels listed above were shipped into this country at Cardiff Docks although six, at least, arrived at Barry Docks.

The first to arrive were Nos. 7961–7980, mostly in December 1943; No. 7965 was the first to go trial — to Rogerstone Yard — on 28th December. From February 1944 onwards, the trials of diesels were invariably to Risca. Only a handful of Ebbw drivers had any diesel experience, and that only on the AEC/GWR railcars, hence it is not certain who drove the US diesels. However, the notebook does reveal that one GWR driver (only identified as Paybill No. 20) accompanied all US diesel trials from Ebbw Junction, thus it can reasonably be assumed that he was specially trained and seconded to these duties for a while, and that he did the driving out on the running lines, with a US Sergeant Sapper accompanying him. He was obviously on hand for the passing out of the locomotive and to give assistance should it be required.

The author has not come across any definite evidence that any of the diesels worked a booked train on the main line, despite unconfirmed reports that one or two were tried out on goods trains as far as Gloucester and back. One report even suggested that one of the Whitcombs was put in charge of the North Mail (a passenger working) from Swansea to Neyland on one occasion. However, unless official information comes to light, the author feels that these reports should be treated with caution, as driver "Paybill No. 20" appeared to be far too occupied at Ebbw to be undertaking such duties.

The other Whitcombs, Nos. 8120–8129, were the next to arrive, also at Cardiff Docks, and were at Ebbw Junction by March. Their initial trials took place during the period 23rd March to 21st April, apart from No. 8123 on 8th May. However, most of the diesels were shown as having second and even third trials, although it would appear that these runs were more to keep the engines in trim than a trial of the locomotive, as the locomotives usually worked in tandem.

Many of the diesels remained stored in the Ebbw Junction area during the summer of 1944, although one or two may have been sent for a spell to the military railways. Six, at least, were sent for storage to the GWR engine shed at Llanelly — Nos. 7971/1/8 and 8120/2/7. It seems they went there in May and returned late July or early August. Once again it is not known how they got to Llanelly, but it seems probable that they were formed into a train, and towed there. The 756 RSB did not station any personnel at Llanelly to look after the engines, but every second Sunday morning a small party was taken there, who examined the engines and took them for a short test run on the single line siding between the shed and Llandilo Junction. Whilst at Llanelly, the US diesels were stored in the rear turntable section of the shed. The Whitcomb diesels were sent to Southampton Docks, late July/early August where they were lifted on to ferries, and shipped to Cherbourg and Le Havre. For some reason one, No. 8121, remained for several weeks more at Ebbw, and was still there on 15th September.

The GEC 380 hp DEs were the next to be dealt with, Nos. 7924–7929 arriving at Ebbw late April. The four recorded trials from this batch, Nos. 7924/5/7/8, all took place during May, some having second runs later. This batch all remained at Ebbw until August, when they left for overseas. Identical diesels Nos. 8499–8509 (with the possible exception of the unrecorded 8504) arrived in May and had their initial trial runs in June. They were usually worked in tandem, i.e. the three trial runs recorded for 9th June were Nos. 7974+7977, 8506+8508, and 7925+8501. That second batch of 380 hp diesels did not stop at Ebbw long, and most were reported as being shipped from Southampton during July. The last batch of the smaller diesels, Nos. 8521–8528, did not arrive at Ebbw until August, and had their trial runs from 28th August to 1st September inclusive, after which they were quickly despatched for overseas duty.

The GEC 500 hp diesels Nos. 7228–7237 (less possibly 7234/5) arrived at Ebbw in June, No. 7231 being the first to go on trial, to Risca, on 16th June. The others had their initial trial runs during July. This batch was despatched for Ebbw, probably made up into one train, on 12th August. Incidentally No. 7233 was shown as travelling 38 miles on its trial trip on 25th July, and it is just possible that it may be the one that got to Gloucester, even if light engine, but that is pure conjecture.

Some similar diesels Nos. 8458/63/4 were reported in the South Wales area on 23rd November, but by that time the 756 RSB had long since left Ebbw Junction and it is probable that the four were being towed from the landing port direct to a South Coast port for re-embarkation, and not calling in at any workshop. This often happened to arrivals in this country, after the allies had secured a firm foothold on the Continent. For instance, 2–8–0s Nos. 5838–5840 and 6062 were reported to have been landed at Avonmouth Dock as late as 4th June, 1945, and towed directly to Dover for re-shipment to France.

A job well done

By early September 1944 the 756 RSB had dealt with over 500 locomotives at Ebbw shop, comprising 358 of the 2–8–0s, at least 104 of the 0–6–0Ts along with some 56 diesels. In addition they had repaired one GWR engine "Aberdare" class 2–6–0 No. 2625, which was used by the US Air force for aerial target practice in West Wales, in May 1944, that repair being carried out under the supervision of the chief boiler inspector of the GWR. By September the second phase of the 756 RSB operations at Ebbw had started: the release from storage of the locomotives under their control (both steam and diesel) with spot checks to ensure that all was well prior to despatch to embarkation port.

This was quickly followed by the receipt of and checking most of the engines that had been working on the GWR. Dealing with the 2–8–0s first, 127 are known to have been sent to Ebbw, for checks and maintenance, plus the remains of No. 1688 which was sent to Ebbw from Swindon in wagons on 9th October. This locomotive had suffered a smashed left-hand cylinder and, with no spares available, its boiler was removed and fitted to No. 2403 on which the firebox crown had collapsed. This was almost certainly the last

No. 2625 in steam after the mock attack, still in its white-washed state and showing the bullet holes in the tender.
British Rail

engine (or part engine to be precise) booked to the 756 RSB at Ebbw Junction as the battalion vacated the premises a couple of weeks later. The 2–8–0s which had been on loan to the GWR began to arrive at Ebbw on 6th September (Nos. 1617/41, 1884/92, 2150, 2294, 2338/54 and 2442) and, apart from the remains of No. 1688, the last to arrive were Nos. 1601, 1616 and 1619 on 7th October. Apart from those returned from the GWR, eight at least of those on loan to the LNER were also sent there. These were Nos. 1833/4/6, 2048, 2150 and 2300/2/37. As the LNER returns were only recorded sketchily it is probable that many more arrived from that source but, unless Major Hanly's daily record book ever turns up, this cannot be confirmed. Once again so many engines were arriving at Ebbw for the USA/TC within a few days that the two pre-shop storage sites were used again, and I saw several of the 2–8–0s at Three Bridges sidings.

I have already mentioned that the 0–6–0Ts on loan to the GWR were all back at Ebbw Junction by 8th September and these were followed by many others from various parts of the country, for a final check/maintenance, prior to despatch for overseas. The notebook only recorded nineteen of these, Nos. 1260/3/5/83, 1392/5, 1401/6/9/23/6 and 1942/3/54/6/8/63/7/72, but the real total is believed to have been considerably higher, probably 40 to 50. Some of these were lettered "WD" the others "USA Transportation Corps". On 19th September I saw Nos. 1401 and 1406 lettered "WD" and No. 1939 with 4383 lettered "USA-TC".

It is unlikely that the final total of engines dealt with by the 756 RSB between September 1943 and October 1944 will ever be known, but a reasonably reliable estimate is:

Section A — *Prepare, trial and store*

2–8–0	358
0–6–0T	104 (Probably 112)
0–4–4–0DE	56 (Probably 61)

Section B — *Final check, and prepare for overseas duty after use in this country*

2–8–0	135 (Probably nearer 175)
0–6–0T	19 (Probably nearer 50)

(Engines in this section do not include any already listed in Section A.)

Section C — *Others*

2–8–0	No. 1688 returned in pieces in wagons
2–6–0	GWR No. 2625 after use as an aerial target for the USA-AF
0–4–0D	Diesel shunter No. D5 (USA-TC)

This makes a definite total of 675, with a grand total far more likely to have been in the region of 750. Although the work on each engine was not excessive, the number of dead engine movements was huge, particularly as a good deal of this was in the cramped fitting shop yard sited between the

GWR shed entrances and yard, and the coal stacking dump for the depot*. It was a magnificent achievement by Major Hanly and his men, not only in dealing with such a large number of locomotives — both steam and diesel — in the thirteen months the 756 RSB occupied the fitting shop at Ebbw Junction, but also supervising the storage sites at Tonteg, Penrhos, Cadoxton and Duffryn Isaf, and also keeping an eye on the Whitcomb diesels at Llanelly shed. It was not just a matter of guarding the engines at the storage sites, they had to be regularly inspected, and greased and oiled as necessary to ensure they were in first class condition when the call came for their despatch overseas.

The Battalion left Ebbw Junction towards the end of October 1944, and regrouped the following month at Marseilles in Southern France. According to a report in the excellent book on the *USA Transportation Corps*, the Battalion spent their spell in Europe preparing American built box wagons for use on the Continental railways, mainly to replace the numerous local losses sustained during the German retreat. It is recorded that they dealt with no less than 28,801 wagons, another remarkable achievement.

The fitting shop at Ebbw Junction reverted back to GWR control, and resumed its former role as the depot for light, non-factory, repairs for engines located, or working, in the Newport Division. Twenty-one years afterwards, as from 11th October, 1965, the depot closed entirely and was quickly demolished. New maintenance and servicing sheds for diesel locomotives were erected a short distance westwards of the old shed and fitting shop, partly on the site of the old US yard of 1943/4. The new maintenance shed opened on 5th December, 1965, and the servicing shed on 29th May, 1966. Both had a comparatively short life and, despite the introduction of certain wagon repairs for a period to provide extra work, the depot closed in August 1982, except as a signing-on point. It finally closed entirely as from 29th December, 1983 on which date the remaining men were transferred to Newport High Street, again for signing-on purposes.

Likewise most of the railways used for the former US storage sites have long-since disappeared. For a while the running lines at Tonteg reverted to normal up and down double line working, but the section closed entirely in June 1951. At Penrhos the sidings remained for railway domestic use until the last section of the old Barry Railway's Rhymney branch (which passed through the sidings) was taken out of use on 14th December, 1967. The main line from Barry to Cardiff remains in regular use, but the sidings used to store the 'S160' 2-8-0s were taken up, after cessation of the coal trade, in the mid-1960s. The B&M line north of Bedwas (somewhat similar to the Tonteg storage site in that it ran on a ledge cut into the eastern hillside of the Rhymney Valley) which fanned out for the Duffryn Isaf sidings, was closed to all traffic as from 12th December, 1962, and little trace of the site now remains. Finally Llanelly engine shed closed as from 2nd September, 1965, and the siding from the shed to the main line at Llandilo Junction was taken up soon afterwards.

Thus little now remains to remind one of that brief but important part of the transport history of the last War.

---

* See Appendix Three for comprehensive details of the problems faced by the GWR at Ebbw Jn, because of the "USA activity" there.

Appendix One
2–8–0 Storage Sites

Tonteg Site
   First Arrivals: 11th October, 1943, 2606 (Tunnel end) + 2827 + 2599
   Last Arrivals: 8th December, 1943, 2193 + 2804 + 2574 (Tonteg Jn end)
   Total Engines Stored 119

2154–8/60–3/6/8–88/91–3/5–9	39
2232–7/40/56/62/8/71/2/5/6/8/81	16
2320/72/6	3
2449/51–9	10
2500/72/4/8/9/81/3–5/91/3–9	17
2600–14/8	16
2804/6–10/2–21/7/8	18
	119

   Site cleared: 28th August, 1944–7th September, 1944.

Penrhos Site
   First Arrivals: 9th December, 1943, 2257 + 2805 + 2838
   Last Arrivals: 26th February, 1944, 2507 + 2258
   Total Engines Stored 152

1625/6/9–31/3–8/40/52/3/66/77–9/90/1	20
1701/81/90/3/4/6/7	7
1804–8	5
1906	1
2071/2	2
2194	1
2200/1/3–5/8/9/11/3/4/8/30/1/41/54/5/7/8/60/1/6/77	22
2336/41/2/7	4
2501–5/7–9/12/26/38–45/60–7/9/70/3/5/80/2/6/8/9/92	36
2615–7/20/2/3/5/32/4/6–8/40–4	17
2805/11/22–5/9/31–3/5/7–45/62/3/6/7/9–72/92/3	30
2901/8/9/17/24/8/9	7
	152

   Nos. 1640, 1804, 2204, 2565, 2588/9, 2643/4 & 2866 left 2nd–5th May, 1944.
   Remainder of site cleared c.9th–21st August, 1944.

Cadoxton Site
   First Arrivals: 1st March, 1944, 2926 + 2568 + 2910 + 2537
   Last Arrivals: May 1944, 2337 and 2868
   Probable Total Engines Stored 84

1627/80/5/6	4
1756/89/91/5/8	5
2202/6/7/10/5/59/63/5	8
2330/1/3–5/7/40/3–6	11
2506/10/1/3–9/33–7/46–9/68/71/6/7/87	24

APPENDIX

2619/24/33/5/45	5
2778–81	4
2830/4/47/68/94–7	8
2900/2–7/10–3/20/3/6/7	15
	84

Doubtful case: No. 2571 left for overseas 2nd May, 1944 and it is possible it remained at Ebbw Jn and not put to store.
Site cleared: 26th August, 1944–2nd September, 1944.

Other 'S160' class 2–8–0s initially prepared at Ebbw Jn
    2639   Completed and sent to Longmoor Military Ry January 1944
    2264 and 2858 Completed April 1944 and despatched for overseas duty 2nd May, 1944.

Appendix Two
Return of 2–8–0s on Loan to GWR

To USA/TC Ebbw Jn: 127+1 in pieces (6th September, 1944 to 7th October, 1944 inclusive)
    1601–4/7–10/5–20/2–4/8/32/9/41/5–8/51/5/6/61–5/82/7
    1749/57
    1835/41/77/81/4/91/2/7–9
    1900–2/9/10/4/5
    2096/8
    2100/2/3/16/8/22/9–38/41/2/4/5/7–51/9/64/5
    2270/80/94
    2312–5/8/9/23/6/7/38/9/50–4/7/9/60/8/9/75/7
    2404/7/10/22/4/30–4/8–42/8/50
    Also remains of No. 1688 in wagons 9th October, 1944.

To Cardiff Docks for Shipment: 20 (25th–28th September, 1944 inclusive)
    1605/6/11/54/81/9
    1883/93,1913
    2112/67, 2267/9/79
    2358, 2403/8/23/35/43

To Eastleigh Works: 22 (9th–21st September, 1944 inclusive)
    1612–4/21/44/9/59/60/83/4
    1880/94–6, 2110/39/40/3
    2290, 2324/49, 2405

Return Depot not Recorded: 4
    1642 (20th Sept., 1944), 1643 (27th Sept., 1944), 1658 (20th Sept., 1944), 2109 (27th Sept., 1944).

Appendix Three

USA 756 RSB and GWR
Meeting at Ebbw Junction on the 27th January, 1944

Mr Baines stated 370 yards of the "Shop" sidings had been surrendered to the USA authorities. The loss of the use of these sidings, apart from the interference with movements in the Locomotive Yard, was a major cause of the difficulties.

He supported suggestion that extra siding accommodation was required in addition to three sidings now in process of being laid down, but thought that proposed extra sidings may not be necessary if the USA authorities relinquish the use of two or three of the "Shop" Sidings.

Regarding a suggestion that the services of American technicians be employed on GWR work, Mr Baines mentioned they had been told to keep away from the shed and the Shops Steward would probably object to proposal.

Mr Baines was requested to review immediately with American authorities:

(a) Congested state of Shop Sidings.
(b) Presence of many more engines and tanks than can be currently treated.
(c) Effective regulation of traffic according to actual daily needs.
(d) Restoration of as many Shop Sidings as possible (at least two or three) to GWR use.

Mr Baines and Mr Pepler to confer and closely examine matter after the former contacts USA authorities, and agree allocation of alternative siding accommodation in the neighbourhood for USA use, if necessary.

NOTE: Result of meeting between Mr Pepler, Mr Baines and Major Hanly (USA) Thursday, 27th January, 1944.

(i) Agreed weighbridge road and the next but one adjacent to it be handed over to Locomotive Dept.
(ii) 8 tank wagons to be transferred to A.D. Junction sidings and, in future, tank wagons to be worked from Maesglas to A.D. Junction Sidings and not to Ebbw Shops.
(iii) Major Hanly has arranged for compressor and tools to be transferred to A.D. Junction Sidings.
(iv) SHUNTING — in future, traffic to be worked to USA Shops as directed by Foreman or Assistant. In all cases in future, engines from outside Newport District to be conveyed to local stabling ground for subsequent transfer to Ebbw Shops at suitable times.
(v) Pilot trips 10.30 am and 4.00 pm daily to work traffic to and from Shops and Yard.
(vi) Major Hanly will instruct his staff that they must obey instructions of man on ground when performing shunting movements.

Employment of Italian Prisoners of War.
Mr Baines had asked for 10 of these men and thought the nearest camp

was at Llanvaches (approximately 10 miles from Newport — about three miles north of Magor). He understood there was a similar camp at St Lawrence (query Chepstow).

Agreed that use could be made of 50 Italian PoW at Severn Tunnel and Ebbw Junction Locomotive Sheds if Headquarters agreed to proposal.

NOTE: Since ascertained from Major Raikes, Movement Control, Abergavenny that at present the Camp nearest to Newport is that in the Abergavenny area (distance about 18 miles). The Major stated that if appropriate Military authority is given for employment of these men, in the Newport or Severn Tunnel area, a camp, with hostel, would in all probability be established at a suitable location within easy reach of either place.

Italian PoW Camps are also located at:

Llanvihangel	26 miles from Newport
Peterchurch	(Herefordshire)
Dorstone	(Herefordshire)
Crickhowell	(Brecs.)
Coleford	(Gloucestershire)
Sudely Castle	(Gloucestershire)
etc. etc.	

Callers Up — Use of Motor Bicycles.

Callers Up included 22 women and, owing to absenteeism, etc. it was not unusual for members of the Shed and Yard staff to be taken away from essential work to call up Drivers, Firemen and Guards.

Mr Baines thought the provision of three motor-cycles would certainly be advantageous.

Breakdown Gangs

Shed Fitters and other staff concerned directly or indirectly with preparation of engines make up breakdown gangs. Number of derailments, etc. resulted in Shed staff being depleted rather frequently.

Mr Baines undertook to furnish statement showing number of times breakdown gangs called out during October, November, December, 1943 together with average strength and constitution of gangs. Recently, derailments had averaged three a week and it was stated 138 (query) had occurred in one month.

Mr Dymond pointed out this was another reason for demanding optimum staff requirements for the establishment.

Mr Page said that at the particular time 8 to 10 engines were waiting to be washed out, and considered that if two or three long sidings, covered over, were available, such accommodation would be most beneficial, particularly for washouts. He maintained that such extra covered siding accommodation would assist more than anything else. At present engines requiring this treatment occupy valuable siding space in the Yard until berths are available in the shed.

The "Platform" Road in the Yard is the only siding available for stabling engines waiting washouts, fitters' attention etc. This is totally inadequate with the consequence that use has to be made of 2 of the four Firepit sidings which are needed for their designed purpose.

Mr Page added that he had frequently drawn his Superintendent's attention to the fact that the resources of the Shed were overtaxed.

Three new sidings (one fairly long and two short) will be laid down on 30th January and it is anticipated that the work will be completed a few days afterwards. They will be used for stabling wagons of coal, engines, etc. The Shed Foreman felt that more accommodation than this was necessary, if there was to be freedom of movement. In any case these three new sidings were not suitably located for engine stabling.

"USA" Shops

Hours of work 8.00 am to 5.00 pm weekdays (to 12.00 Saturdays). Shops idle from 12.00 noon Saturdays to 8.00 am Mondays.

Potential source of labour during weekends.

12 sidings form the Shop sidings.

10 berths inside Shops used exclusively by the USA authorities and two berths are allocated for GWR use for dealing with GWR engines with hot boxes or other fairly long jobs. This arrangement affords negligible relief inasmuch as we can only put two of our engines in the Shop.

Interior of Shops and the 12 sidings outside are invariably fully occupied with USA engines, tanks, etc. — apparently much more than can be dealt with currently by the USA personnel. On Tuesday, 25th January, at 5.00 pm, 23 USA engines and four tank cars occupied practically the whole of the siding accommodation, whilst another trip of USA engines and tank cars was about to be put off in this nest of sidings.

Shed Foreman stated that booked trips were earmarked for working traffic to and from the Shop Sidings and the Guards take instructions from the USA people as to what is to be brought in from the stabling sidings at Park Jn and West Mendalgief.

Agreed that an effective system of regulation of inwards traffic be instituted as quickly as possible, and that Guards be instructed forthwith that no traffic is to be conveyed from Park Jn and West Mendalgief except as directed by the Shed Foreman or Assistant Shed Foreman.

Shed Foreman instructed to discuss fully with Major Hanly (USA) the question of extent of traffic, i.e. engines and tanks, to be worked to Shop Sidings during each 24 hours, with the object of reducing use of Shop Sidings by USA people to the minimum and leaving at least three of the twelve sidings for the exclusive use of our Locomotive Department. Shed Foreman and Major Hanly to meet at a specified time daily to agree programme for ensuing 24 hours. System of regulation to be agreed.

Mr Page requested to report result of discussions to Mr Baines.

The release of two or three sidings outside the shops would materially ease the position in the Locomotive Yard and shed, and it was felt that the matter was one which should be explored thoroughly.

It was understood that the average daily output from the Shops was four engines per day, and it was not therefore appreciated why the 12 sidings should be more or less constantly cluttered up with a very much larger

number of engines and tank cars than could be attended to each day.
(NOTE: At the meeting at Newport on Wednesday, 26th January, Mr Pepler and Mr Baines were requested to collaborate after Mr Baines had had an opportunity of discussing the subject with the USA Authorities. Matter to be dealt with as a matter of urgency. If needs be, other accommodation to be allocated to the USA people.)

Sand for USA Engines at Shops.

Formerly sand wheeled from back of Shed to Shops. Now USA engines from Shops are brought into the Shed for filling sand boxes with dry sand. This involves unnecessary movements and must be avoided. Mr Page instructed to see Major Hanly and make alternative arrangements.

Carriage Sheds

In view of the rather remote position of Ebbw Jn Carriage Sheds in relation to the Locomotive Shed it was doubted whether the use of the former for washing out engines etc., would on the whole be beneficial, although the work could be performed there. Additional movements to and from the Yard and Shed would be entailed and at a focal point.

There are three sidings on *each* side of coal stage provided for fire-dropping, coaling and ashloading, viz.

Firepit and coal stage siding	Used as such
Ashloading siding	Used as such
*Firepit siding	Not used as such

* Used to stable engines requiring boiler washing, mechanical treatment, repairs, etc. or engines which cannot be accommodated in the Shed or in appropriate place in Yard.

In effect this means that 50% of firepit siding accommodation not utilised for purposes laid down. If engines could have their fires dropped on these two firepit sidings, the engines could be set back on coal stage siding for coaling from the Shed and without difficulty.

Use of these two "unused" firepit sidings would obviously entail employment of more men.

This feature emphasises need for extra siding accommodation in the Locomotive Yard.

Interference with Movements to and from Locomotive Yard by Shunting of USA Engines etc. to and from adjoining Ebbw Shops now occupied by USA Authorities.

This is a most disturbing factor, as the shunting to and fro of USA engines and wagons of USA Stores is right across the path of engines going on to the firepit and coalstage sidings and of engines on the way out from Shed.

Need for continuous supervision of Yard working is all the more imperative on this account, if all shunting etc. movements are to be properly regulated in the interests of expedition.

Assistant Shift Foreman on each turn spends as much time as possible directing the operations in the Yard, but he can only devote a part of his time to this work, whereas continuous supervision is essential. Shed Foreman sometimes spends an hour or so watching the movements.

Our operations would be facilitated if the Locomotive and Shop sections of the Yards could be used for the purposes for which they were designed. USA traffic and increase in number of engines dealt with at Ebbw Jn Shed imposes an undue burden and overtaxes resources.

Operations in Shed

Tubes are cleaned in the Shed, regardless of Home Depot of engine. "Booked" blocked tubes are attended to. Unbooked blocked tubes are only given attention if they are subsequently discovered to be blocked.

Ordinary process is to blow steam through tubes. Other method is to run rods through tubes — outgoing drivers frequently ask for this to be done before they will take over.

Loading railway rolling stock for France on to train ferries at a southern port in England.

The Southern Railway steamer *Twickenham Ferry* was the first to discharge a cargo of rolling stock on the Cherbourg Peninsula; it consisted of a complete train of goods wagons with locomotive. *Above* is seen a 50-year-old French locomotive with French driver towing a 65-ton diesel-electric locomotive ashore on the Cherbourg Peninsula. Right is Captain S. Hancock, D.S.O., Master of the *Twickenham Ferry* and *below* is a further view of the American diesel locomotive being off-loaded from the Twickenham Ferry in August 1944.

Locomotive Magazine

Appendix Four

Specification of USA Locomotives seen at Newport

US Army 0–6–0T

Leading Dimensions
Cylinders (2): 16½" dia. 24" stroke
Wheels, 4' 6" dia.
Boiler Pressure, 210 lb. per sq.in.
Tractive Effort, 21,600 lb.
Weight, 46 T 10 C.
Bunker, 1 T. coal.
Tanks, 1,200 gallons.
No superheater.

Built by H.K. Porter & Co., Pittsburgh.
Vulcan Iron Works, Wilkes-Barre.
Davenport Locomotive Works, Iowa.

For shunting purposes in Army Depots and Port Areas, a small "Austerity" engine of the 0–6–0 Tank type was designed and built in the United States for the Transportation Corps.

A number of these locomotives were lent to the British War Department and carried WD markings, although they were still numbered in the US number series.

In addition to those in Depots and Port Areas in this country, many were in service in Western Europe, North Africa and Italy.

Engine Numbers and Builders:
US Nos. 1250–1499
    1927–1999
    4300–4399
    6000–6090

BUILDERS

H.K. Porter & Co.	Vulcan Loco. Works	Davenport Loco. Works
1250–1269	1270–1289	1300–1319
1290–1299	1450–1499	1927–1951
1320–1399	1952–1999	4374–4399
1400–1449	4331–4373	6000–6049
4300–4330		
6050–6090		

US Army 0-4-4-0 Diesel Electric

0-4-4-0 Diesel Electric, designed and built by the Whitcomb Locomotive Co., Rochelle, USA.

Two supercharged "Buda" Diesel units each driving "Westinghouse" generators which in turn furnish power for two traction motors.

Weight, 80 T. 650 hp.

Similar, except for loading gauge, to those taken over by the British Ministry of Supply. Service in Western Europe.

These Diesel electric locomotives built by the Whitcomb Locomotive Co., for the US Transportation Corps were of a similar, but more recent, design to those built by this firm for the Ministry of Supply in 1941.

After the success of those built for Britain, the US Army Transportation Corps adopted this design for all its larger Diesel locomotives. Consequently, this design was seen on nearly all the US fronts in the war, the double bogie design enabling it to traverse the very sharp curves met on most light railways.

The first Allied train to enter Rome on 4th July, 1944, was headed by a Whitcomb Diesel Electric 0-4-4-0.

Engine Numbers: **7900-8575 Built by Whitcomb Loco. Co.**

US Army 2-8-0

Leading Dimensions

Cylinders (2): 19" dia. × 26" stroke
Wheels, Truck, 2' 9" dia.
Wheels, Coupled, 4' 9" dia.
Boiler Pressure, 225 lb. per sq.in.
Tractive Effort, 31,490 lb.
Weight, Engine, 72 T. 10 C.
Weight, Tender, 51 T. 15 C.
 Total, 124 T. 5 C.
Tender, coal, 9 T.
Tender, water, 6,500 gallons.

Designed by Major J.W. Marsh of the US Army Corps of Engineers.
Built by Baldwin Locomotive Works, Philadelphia. Lima Locomotive Works, Lima, Ohio. American Locomotive Works, Schenectady.

A large number of "Austerity" locomotives were ordered by the US Army Transportation Corps for service in Western Europe. Designed by Major Marsh, of the US Army Corps of Engineers, they were of the 2-8-0 type and were built by the three major locomotive firms in the United States.

They were built to the British Loading Gauge for use in this country when traffic was heavily increased by the presence of so many US troops here, before they were sent to the Continent behind the American Armies.

In addition to those in service on the Western Front, many of these locomotives were sent to North Africa and, later, Italy.

Engine Numbers and Builders:
US Nos. 1600–1926
 2000–2929
 3200–3689
 5700–5849

BUILDERS

American Loco. Co.	Baldwin Loco. Co.	Lima Loco. Co.
1600–1676	1677–1826	1827–1926
2000–2151	2242–2379	2152–2241
2380–2459	2590–2775	2500–2589
2804–2929	3380–3559	2776–2803
3200–3379		3560–3599
		3600–3689
		5700–5849

American Freight Locomotives

CAB FITTINGS OF U.S.A. S160 CLASS, 2—8—0 LOCOMOTIVE.

1. Regulator handle.
2. Reversing lever.
3. Vacuum auto. brake lever.
4. Steam valve, small ejector.
5. Steam brake lever.
6. Whistle pulls.
7. L.H. injector steam valve.
8. Blower steam valve.
9. Steam sander valve.
10. Steam brake valve.
11. Steam shut off valve turret.
12. Vacuum brake steam valve.
13. Mechanical lubricator steam valve.
14. Air pump steam valve.
15. R.H. injector steam valve.
16. Blower control valve.
17. Coal watering cock and hose.
18. Water gauge.
19. Water gauge drain valve.
20. Water gauge bottom stop valve.
21. Water gauge rod to top stop valve.
22. Boiler pressure gauge.
23. Westinghouse brake gauge.
24. Vacuum brake gauge.
25. Firehole door.
26. Firegrate rocking levers.
27. Injector water and overflow valves.
28. Injector operating levers.
29. Driver's seat.
30. Locker and fireman's seat.
31. Flag box.
32. Steam sanding lever.
33. Three water level test cocks.
34. Cylinder cock lever.
35. Westinghouse brake lever.
36. Steam brake lubricator.

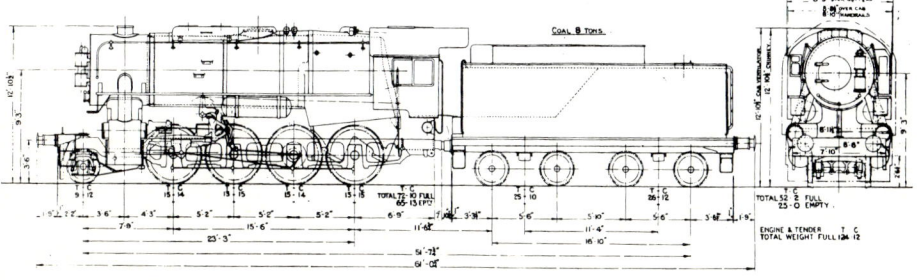

ENGINE DIAGRAM GIVING PRINCIPAL DIMENSIONS.

CYLINDERS.—Diam., 19″; Stroke, 26″.
BOILER.—Barrel, 12′ 11⅜″; Diam. Outside, 5′ 8⅜″ and 5′ 10″.
FIREBOX.—Outside, 7′ 9⅝″ by 6′ 7″; Inside, 7′ 0¼″ by 5′ 10¼″. Height, 5′ 6½″ by 4′ 6⅝″.
TUBES.—Fire Tubes, No. 30; Diam., 5⅜″; No. 150; Diam. 2″; Length, 13′ 6″.
HEATING SURFACE.—Superheater Tubes, 480 sq. ft. Fire Tubes, 1,637 sq. ft. Firebox, 136 sq. ft. Total, 2,253 sq. ft.
AREA OF FIREGRATE.—41.0 sq. ft.
WHEELS.—Pony, 2′ 9″; Coupled, 4′ 9″.
WATER CAPACITY OF TENDER.—5,400 gallons.
WORKING PRESSURE :—225 lbs. sq. in.
TRACTIVE EFFORT.—31,500 lbs.
TOTAL WEIGHT OF ENGINE.—72 tons 10 cwt. full. 65 tons 13 cwt. empty.
TOTAL WEIGHT OF TENDER.—52 tons 2 cwt. full. 25 tons 0 cwt. empty.

US Army 2-8-2

Leading Dimensions

Cylinders (2): 16" dia. 24" stroke
Wheels, Truck, 2' 6" dia.
Wheels, Coupled, 4' dia.
Boiler Pressure, 185 lb. per sq.in.
Tractive Effort, 20,100 lb.
Weight, Engine, 52 T.
Weight, Tender, 43 T.
   Total, 95 T.
Tender, coal, 9 T.
Tender, water, 5,000 gallons.
Gauge, metre

Built by Baldwin Locomotive Works, Philadelphia. Davenport Locomotive Works, Iowa.

A large number of locomotives of the 2–8–2 type were built for the US Transportation Corps for service in the Far Eastern War Theatre.

Built in the United States they saw service in India, Burma and the Philippines.

Engine Numbers: 200–299 Built by Baldwin Loco. Co.
                 300–399 Built by Davenport Loco. Works

American Built 0–4–4–0 Diesel Electric Locomotive

Leading Dimensions
0–4–4–0 Diesel Electric, designed and built by the Whitcomb Locomotive Co., Rochelle, USA. Two supercharged "Buda" Diesel units each driving Westinghouse Generators which in turn furnish power for two traction motors.

Weight, 65 T., 600 horse-power.

    The Whitcomb Locomotive Co., of USA, designed and built these double bogie Diesel electric locomotives in 1941. Over one hundred were purchased by the War Department and sent to the Middle East.
    Owing to lack of water in the Western Desert, they were chiefly used on the Mersa Matruh run — steam motive power being used as far as Mersa Matruh from Alexandria.
    Some of the later locomotives were armoured as a protection against attacks by low flying aircraft.
    Many were also used by the British in Iran.

Engine Numbers: **1200–1259**
                           1300–1369

Appendix Five

Serious Accidents with USA Locomotives

There were three serious accidents involving American locomotives. In each case the crown of the steel firebox collapsed, due to a shortage of water in the boiler.

The first case, on 17th November, 1943, occurred at Honeybourne, GWR. Just before midnight a freight train was running at about 25 mph when the locomotive's firebox crown collapsed*; the fireman, who was firing at the time, was so badly scalded by escaping steam and water that he died later in the day. The driver was much more fortunate and received such slight injuries that he did not even have to go off duty. It was determined that the men had been misled by a false indication in the single water gauge, resulting from the steam valve of the gauge being only partially open. Unlike the plug cocks fitted to British engines, where the position of the handle revealed whether it was fully open or not, the screw valves fitted to American engines had to be tested to indicate their position. Furthermore, the lead plugs in the firebox crown which should have melted to indicate that a dangerous situation was being reached, failed to do so, which was found to be a design fault and new plugs were fitted.

Following Honeybourne, comprehensive instructions as to the purpose of the water gauge and test cocks (the latter replaced the second water gauge normal in this country and were to prove the level of water in the gauge) were issued to enginemen in all companies employing USA locomotives. Unfortunately, they had not reached the men who were in charge of an American engine hauling a lightly loaded night freight train at Thurston, LNER on 12th January, 1944. In very similar circumstances, the firebox crown again collapsed blowing the fireman right off the footplate. Fortunately he escaped with bruises, burns and shock, although the driver sustained more serious injuries including a broken thigh and burns. Once again it was found that the steam valve to the water gauge had only been partially open.

The final case was the worst of all in that both the driver and fireman were killed. A lightly loaded freight train was passing through South Harrow tunnel, LNER, at about 2.45 am on 30th October, 1944 when the firebox crown of the American engine collapsed, due to shortage of water in the boiler. Probably because the train was confined within a tunnel, the effects on the footplate were more severe and both men succumbed to their injuries. In this case the men were completely familiar with the engine, and each had signed a document stating that he had seen the notices regarding the water gauge and test cocks. The shortage of water appeared to have been due to some mismanagement on the part of the enginemen.

No further serious accidents are recorded and by the time of the last one the engines were being withdrawn for service overseas.

---

* This may have been locomotive No. 2403 (see *page 30*).